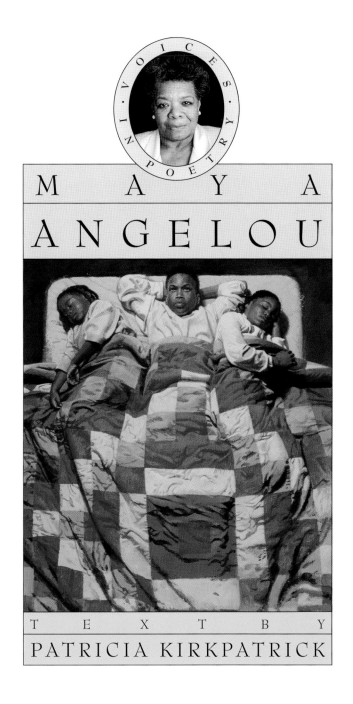

VOICES · IN · POETRY

M A Y A
ANGELOU

T E X T   B Y
PATRICIA KIRKPATRICK

ILLUSTRATIONS BY
JOHN THOMPSON

CREATIVE EDUCATION

*Y*ou may write me down in history
With your bitter, twisted lies,
You may trod me in the very dirt
But still, like dust, I'll rise.

Does my sassiness upset you?
Why are you beset with gloom?
'Cause I walk like I've got oil wells
Pumping in my living room.

Just like moons and like suns,
With the certainty of tides,
Just like hopes springing high,
Still I'll rise.

Did you want to see me broken?
Bowed head and lowered eyes?
Shoulders falling down like teardrops,
Weakened by my soulful cries?

Does my haughtiness offend you?
Don't you take it awful hard
'Cause I laugh like I've got gold mines
Diggin' in my own backyard.

You may shoot me with your words,
You may cut me with your eyes,

You may kill me with your hatefulness,
But still, like air, I'll rise.

Does my sexiness upset you?
Does it come as a surprise
That I dance like I've got diamonds
At the meeting of my thighs?

Out of the huts of history's shame
I rise
Up from a past that's rooted in pain
I rise
I'm a black ocean, leaping and wide,
Welling and swelling I bear in the tide.

Leaving behind nights of terror and fear
I rise
Into a daybreak that's wondrously clear
I rise
Bringing the gifts that my ancestors gave,
I am the dream and the hope of the slave.
I rise
I rise
I rise.

From And Still I Rise

INTRODUCTION

"*I believe all things are possible for a human being, and I don't think there's anything in the world I can't do.*"

—Maya Angelou

For American poet Maya Angelou, these words are not spoken easily. Angelou grew up black and poor during the Depression, and was uprooted repeatedly. Although her writing has brought her the world's praise, she did not publish her first book of poetry until she was in her 40s. But she has believed in the beauty and power of language ever since she read poetry as a girl in Stamps, Arkansas. She has pursued that belief not only in poetry, but also by writing autobiography and by performing as a singer, dancer, and actress. In all of her creative endeavors, she raises a spirited voice that honors the hardships suffered under racial injustice yet also mocks oppression and envisions overcoming it. By writing from her life experience in the language of a black woman, she has influenced a generation of African-American writers and helped readers of all races believe that, indeed, all things may be possible for a human being.

Maya Angelou, c. 1970.

SONG FOR THE OLD ONES

*M*y Fathers sit on benches
    their flesh counts every plank
    the slats leave dents of darkness
deep in their withered flanks.

They nod like broken candles
    all waxed and burnt profound
    they say "It's understanding
that makes the world go round."

There in those pleated faces
    I see the auction block
    the chains and slavery's coffles
the whip and lash and stock.

My Fathers speak in voices
    that shred my fact and sound
    they say "It's our submission
that makes the world go round."

They used the finest cunning
    their naked wits and wiles
    the lowly Uncle Tomming
and Aunt Jemimas' smiles.

They've laughed to shield their crying
    then shuffled through their dreams
    and stepped 'n' fetched a country
to write the blues with screams.

I understand their meaning
    it could and did derive
    from living on the edge of death
They kept my race alive.

From *Oh Pray My Wings Are Gonna Fit Me Well*

STAMPS, ARKANSAS

$\mathcal{M}$aya Angelou was born Marguerite Johnson in Saint Louis, Missouri, in 1928. By the time she was three years old, her parents had separated, and she and her older brother were living in California with their father. Unable to raise the children on his own, Maya's father soon sent them by train to live with their grandmother.

> We had arrived in the musty little town, wearing tags on our wrists which instructed—"To Whom It May Concern"—that we were Marguerite and Bailey Johnson Jr., from Long Beach, California, en route to Stamps, Arkansas, c/o Mrs. Annie Henderson.

Maya and her brother stepped off the train into life in a small southern town during the Depression. People were poor, and black people, living under the laws of segregation, were often the poorest of all.

Maya's grandmother was a strict taskmaster who for 25 years ran the only general store in Stamps that catered to black people. Maya often worked behind the counter of the Store, where she witnessed the hardship of people's lives. One of her most striking memories is the night her grandmother hid her uncle Willie in a vegetable bin when the Ku Klux Klan threatened to ride through town and lynch black men. "We were told to take the potatoes and onions out of their bins and knock out the dividing walls that kept them apart. Then with a tedious and fearful slowness Uncle Willie gave me his rubber-tipped cane and bent down to get into the now-enlarged empty bin. . . . we covered him with potatoes and onions, layer upon layer, like a casserole." The hooded Klansmen did not ride that night, and Uncle Willie was not harmed, but Maya never forgot that and other terrors of her childhood.

English poet and playwright William Shakespeare.

American poet and writer Langston Hughes.

Of course in Stamps she also witnessed the beauty, humor, and dignity of daily life in a rural community. And although she often felt inadequate, she was a good student and a passionate reader; she writes that in Stamps she "met and fell in love with William Shakespeare." She also claimed Edgar Allen Poe, Langston Hughes, and Paul Laurence Dunbar among her favorite writers. But she certainly didn't imagine then becoming a writer herself.

*E*ach year I watched the field across from the Store turn caterpillar green, then gradually frosty white. I knew exactly how long it would be before the big wagons would pull into the front yard and load on the cotton pickers at daybreak to carry them to the remains of slavery's plantations.

During the picking season my grandmother would get out of bed at four o'clock (she never used an alarm clock) and creak down to her knees and chant in a sleep-filled voice, "Our Father, thank you for letting me see this New Day. . . ."

Before she had quite arisen, she called our names and issued orders, and pushed her large feet into home-made slippers and across the bare lye-washed wooden floor to light the coal-oil lamp.

The lamplight in the Store gave a soft make-believe feeling to our world which made me want to whisper and walk about on tiptoe. The odors of onions and oranges and kerosene had been mixing all night and wouldn't be disturbed until the wooden slat was removed from the door and the early morning air forced its way in with the bodies of people who had walked miles to reach the pickup place. . . .

In those tender mornings the Store was full of laughing, joking, boasting and bragging. One man was going to pick two hundred pounds of cotton, and another three hundred. Even the children were promising to bring home fo' bits and six bits. . . .

Brought back to the Store, the pickers would step out of the backs of trucks and fold down, dirt-disappointed, to the ground. No matter how much they had picked, it wasn't enough. Their wages wouldn't even get them out of debt to my grandmother, not to mention the staggering bill that waited on them at the white commissary downtown.

From *I Know Why the Caged Bird Sings*

San Francisco, California, in the early 1950s.

SAN FRANCISCO

$\mathcal{E}$ventually, Maya and Bailey went to live with their mother, first in Saint Louis and then in San Francisco. Tragically, when she was eight years old, Maya was raped by her mother's boyfriend. The man was apprehended and convicted but then mysteriously released from jail. A few days later he was found dead. Maya, the victim of a horrible crime, was deeply traumatized. She did not speak aloud for almost five years.

She did continue to read and study. Graduating at the top of her eighth grade class, she attended George Washington High School in San Francisco. She credits the attention of a particular teacher there for helping her to believe in herself and the importance of her education. San Francisco too contributed to her growing sense of self. As a black girl "stalled by the South and Southern Black life style, the city was a state of beauty and a state of freedom. The fog wasn't simply the steamy vapors off the bay caught and penned in by hills, but a soft breath of anonymity that shrouded and cushioned the bashful traveler. I became dauntless and free of fears. . . . In San Francisco, for the first time, I perceived myself as part of something." She writes that she didn't so much identify with other newcomers, blacks, or Asians, but with the "times and the city." World War II was raging. Yet for Angelou, "the undertone of fear that San Francisco would be bombed, which was abetted by weekly air raid warnings, and civil defense drills in school, heightened my sense of belonging."

At the age of 14, Maya Angelou became the first black woman to conduct a streetcar in San Francisco, working split shifts so she could continue her high school classes. At 16, she left a note on her mother's pillow. It read: "Dear Parents, I am sorry to bring this disgrace on the family, but I am pregnant."

A GOOD WOMAN FEELING BAD

*T*he blues may be the life you've led

Or midnight hours in

An empty bed. But persecuting

Blues I've known

Could stalk

Like tigers, break like bone,

Pend like rope in

A gallows tree,

Make me curse

My pedigree,

Bitterness thick on

A rankling tongue,

A psalm to love that's

Left unsung,

Rivers heading north

But ending South,

Funeral music

In a going-home mouth.

All riddles are blues,

And all blues are sad,

And I'm only mentioning

Some blues I've had.

From Shaker, Why Don't You Sing?

M A Y A D E B U T S

While still in high school, Angelou accepted a scholarship to study drama and dance at the California Labor School. Now unmarried and with a newborn son to raise, she needed to make a living. She worked at a number of jobs, including as a waitress and a record store clerk, and after graduating from high school, she turned to dancing. In 1952, at the age of 24, she married a Greek sailor, Tosh Angelous, and took a version of his name for her work as an entertainer. The marriage did not last, but her new name did. Marguerite Johnson became Maya Angelou and moved with her son to New York, where she continued to study dance. Shortly afterward, she got her first big break. She was cast as a singer and dancer in a State Department-sponsored European tour of the opera *Porgy and Bess*. Sadly, she left her young son, Guy, behind in the care of his grandmother, but eventually mother and son were reunited. Angelou married three other times, but she never again changed her name.

Maya Angelou's gift for performance has remained throughout her life and prompted her to pursue various creative forms. A biography of her notes that as "the first black woman director in Hollywood, Angelou has written, produced, directed, and starred in productions for stage, film, and television." As an actress, she was nominated for a Tony for her Broadway debut in *Look Away* and for her performance in *Roots;* she also was nominated for an Emmy for her television performance in *Roots*. Angelou has worked with many talented people, such as writer Alex Haley, actress Diahann Carroll, and television star Oprah Winfrey. In turn, her feeling for the rhythms of spoken language, influenced perhaps by her work as a performer, has been at the heart of Angelou's voice as a poet.

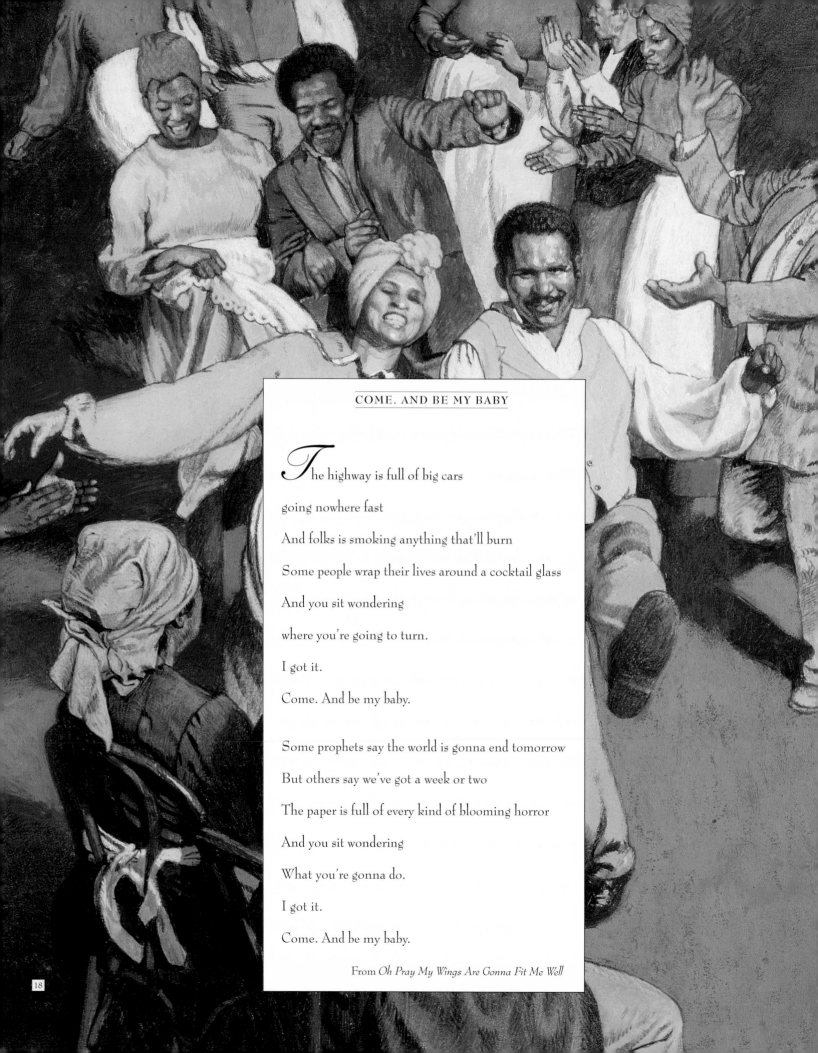

COME. AND BE MY BABY

The highway is full of big cars

going nowhere fast

And folks is smoking anything that'll burn

Some people wrap their lives around a cocktail glass

And you sit wondering

where you're going to turn.

I got it.

Come. And be my baby.

Some prophets say the world is gonna end tomorrow

But others say we've got a week or two

The paper is full of every kind of blooming horror

And you sit wondering

What you're gonna do.

I got it.

Come. And be my baby.

From Oh Pray My Wings Are Gonna Fit Me Well

FREEDOM STRUGGLE

Singing and writing songs brought Angelou's work to the attention of a novelist who urged her to study writing seriously. She joined the Harlem Writer's Guild in New York City. Angelou didn't know if she was good enough to be a writer, but she said later, "I had to try. If I ended in defeat, at least I would be trying. Trying to overcome was black people's honorable tradition."

Trying to overcome racial injustice was Angelou's next pursuit. In 1960, Americans, black and white, were engaged in the civil rights movement. Angelou collaborated with co-

median Godfrey Cambridge to produce the *Cabaret for Freedom,* a musical revue of mostly black performers that played at New York's Village Gate. After the *Cabaret* actors were paid, all revue proceeds went to the Southern Christian Leadership Conference (SCLC), the organization led by Martin Luther King Jr. to non-violently pursue peace, justice, and equality for African Americans. Seeing King speak had inspired Angelou to organize the *Cabaret,* and after the revue closed, she became the northern coordinator for the SCLC. Soon after, she met King face to face.

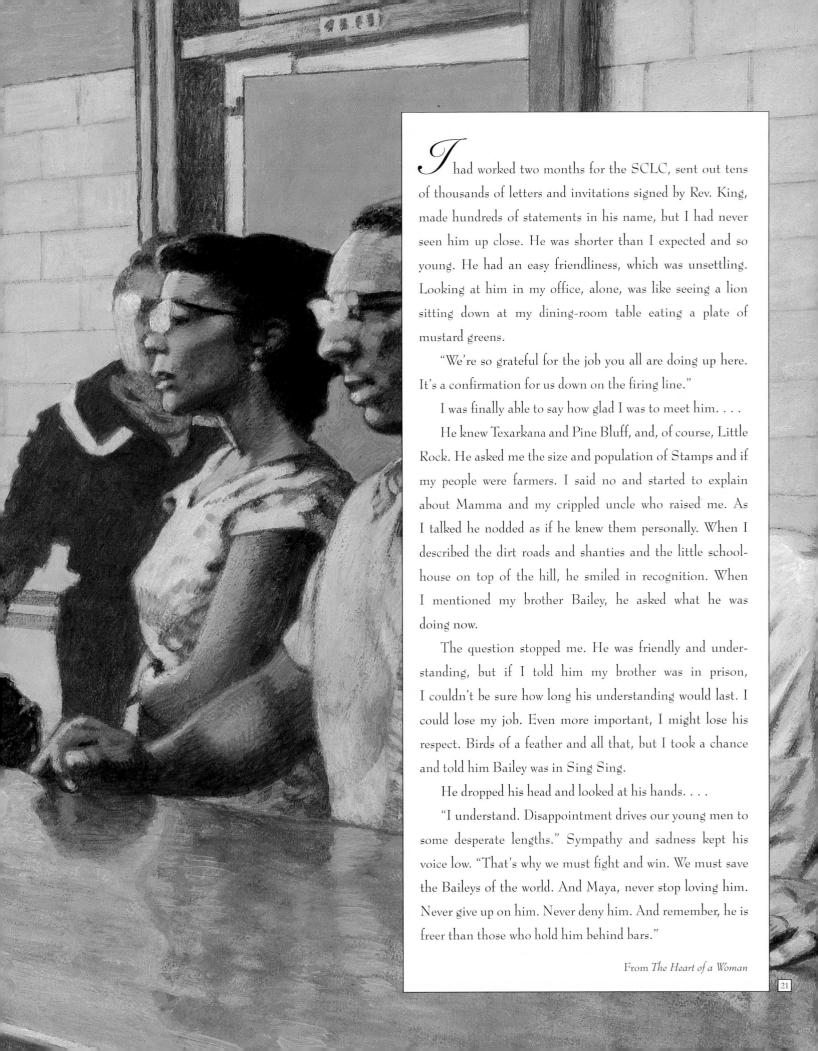

T had worked two months for the SCLC, sent out tens of thousands of letters and invitations signed by Rev. King, made hundreds of statements in his name, but I had never seen him up close. He was shorter than I expected and so young. He had an easy friendliness, which was unsettling. Looking at him in my office, alone, was like seeing a lion sitting down at my dining-room table eating a plate of mustard greens.

"We're so grateful for the job you all are doing up here. It's a confirmation for us down on the firing line."

I was finally able to say how glad I was to meet him. . . .

He knew Texarkana and Pine Bluff, and, of course, Little Rock. He asked me the size and population of Stamps and if my people were farmers. I said no and started to explain about Mamma and my crippled uncle who raised me. As I talked he nodded as if he knew them personally. When I described the dirt roads and shanties and the little school-house on top of the hill, he smiled in recognition. When I mentioned my brother Bailey, he asked what he was doing now.

The question stopped me. He was friendly and under-standing, but if I told him my brother was in prison, I couldn't be sure how long his understanding would last. I could lose my job. Even more important, I might lose his respect. Birds of a feather and all that, but I took a chance and told him Bailey was in Sing Sing.

He dropped his head and looked at his hands. . . .

"I understand. Disappointment drives our young men to some desperate lengths." Sympathy and sadness kept his voice low. "That's why we must fight and win. We must save the Baileys of the world. And Maya, never stop loving him. Never give up on him. Never deny him. And remember, he is freer than those who hold him behind bars."

From The Heart of a Woman

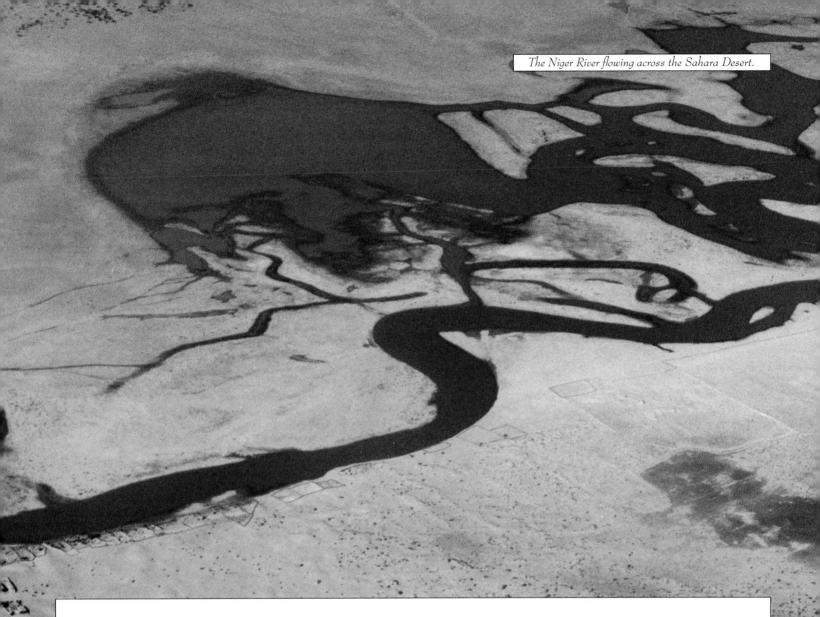

A F R I C A

*I*n 1961, Angelou and her son moved to Africa. They lived at first in Cairo, Egypt, where Guy finished high school and Maya worked as an associate editor for the magazine *The Arab Observer* and learned to speak Arabic. After a year, mother and son decided to move to West Africa. The night their plane flew across the Sahara to their new home, Angelou wept. Her son, thinking she was sorry to leave behind friends in Cairo, handed her Kleenexes.

But the experience of passing over the African continent made Angelou weep for more than her friends; she wept that night for "all my ancestors." She remembered the sleepy mornings and scary nights in her grandmother's store. She recalled the poverty-stricken children she had seen on tenement steps in American cities. Most of all, she realized what suffering the legacy of slavery had meant for her ancestors. "Here, there, along the banks of that river, someone was taken, tied with ropes, shackled with chains, forced to march for weeks carrying the double burden of neck irons and abysmal fear. In that large clump of trees, looking like wood moss from the plane's great height, boys and girls had been hunted like beasts, caught and tethered together."

Later that night, mother and son descended from the plane to the city of Accra, in the country of Ghana. The sights and sounds of the African city both comforted and excited them.

*T*he airport at Accra sounded like an adult playground and looked like a festival. Single travelers, wearing Western suits or dresses which would be deemed fashionable in New York, were surrounded by hordes of well-wishers, swathed in floral prints or the rich plaid silk of Kente cloth. Languages turned the air into clouds of lusty sound. The sight of so many black people stirred my deepest emotions. I had been away from the colors too long. Guy and I grinned at each other and turned to see a sight which wiped our faces clean. Three black men walked past us wearing airline uniforms, visored caps, white pants and jackets whose shoulders bristled with epaulettes. Black pilots? Black captains? It was 1962. In our country, the cradle of democracy, whose anthem boasted "the land of the free, the home of the brave," the only black men in our airports fueled planes, cleaned cabins, loaded food or were skycaps, racing the pavement for tips. Guy nudged me and I turned to see another group of African officers walking unconcerned toward the gate which opened out on the tarmac.

Ghana was the place for my son to go to college. My toby (the Southern black word for a lucky talisman) had "hunched me right." Guy would be able to weigh his intelligence and test his skills without being influenced by racial discrimination.

We passed through customs, delighted to have our bags examined by black people. Our taxi driver was black. The dark night seemed friendly to me, and when the cab's lights illuminated a pedestrian, I saw a black face.

From *The Heart of a Woman*

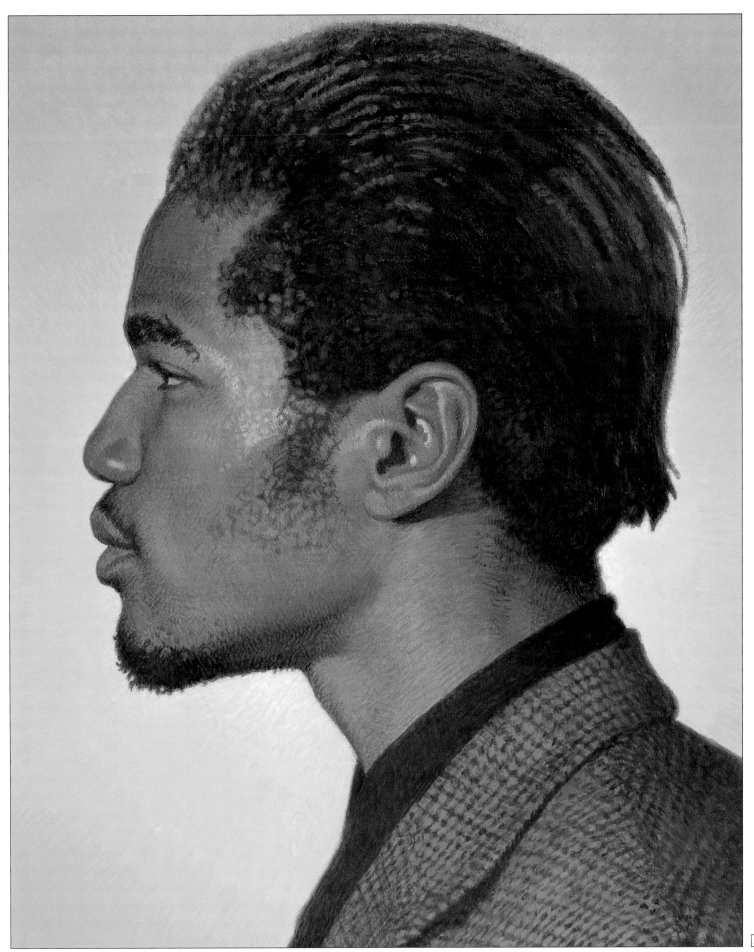

C A G E D   B I R D

After several years in Africa, with her son immersed in his own life at university, Angelou returned to the States and wrote *Blues, Black, Blues,* a television series that explored the influence of African traditions in America. Then, in 1968, just as Angelou was about to begin working for the SCLC again, Martin Luther King Jr. was assassinated. Angelou was devastated. Partly as a way to help her move through her grief, one of Angelou's friends, writer James Baldwin, encouraged her to begin writing her autobiography, which she did. The first volume of the autobiography opens with her arrival in Stamps and goes on to portray her experiences with family and friends as she grew up, went to school, confronted racial prejudice, and began to emerge as a determined young woman.

When it was time to choose a title and theme for the book, Angelou followed the tradition of many other writers who have responded to a past writer's work in their own writing. As a girl, she had loved the black American poet Paul Laurence Dunbar and his poem "Sympathy," which ends with these lines describing the song of a caged bird:

> It's not a carol of joy or glee,
> but a prayer that it sends from its heart's deep core,
> but a plea that upward to heaven it flings.
> I know why the caged bird sings.

Angelou chose Dunbar's line "I know why the caged bird sings" as the title of her book.

Had Angelou herself been a caged bird? After all, an interviewer suggested to her a few years ago, "You've escaped from a cage a few times in your life." "How do you know I did escape?" Angelou responded. "You don't know what demons I still wrestle with. . . . Growing up is admitting that there are demons you cannot overcome." Wrestling with demons became a theme in much of Angelou's writing.

Novelist and essayist James Baldwin.

Civil rights leader Martin Luther King Jr.

Angelou shortly before her first book debuted.

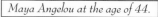

AUTOBIOGRAPHY

*T*o date, Maya Angelou has written six volumes of autobiography. The first, *I Know Why the Caged Bird Sings,* was published in 1970. Nominated for a National Book Award, it became an immediate classic. Like other autobiographies by black women in the 1970s whose goal was "to tell the truth about black women's lives," Angelou's book made an important contribution not only by telling the story of a particular black woman's life but by placing that story within a larger historical moment. "A good autobiographer," Angelou has said, "is writing history from one person's viewpoint." For Angelou, this has meant recreating the historical periods of the Depression, World War II, and the civil rights movement, as well as giving the concrete personal details of what clothes she wore, what city she lived in, and whom she loved.

In addition to autobiography, Angelou has written and published poetry. Her autobiographical volumes, of course, are written in prose sentences, but they often use the rich language and clear images associated with poetry, just as her poetry draws on the autobiographical details of her life. For Angelou, the forms of autobiography and poetry are linked by her strong and spirited writing voice and by her interest in the subjects of work, people, relationships, and struggle. "All my work, my life, everything is about survival," she once said in an interview. "All my work is meant to say, 'You may encounter many defeats, but you must not be defeated.'"

HARLEM HOPSCOTCH

One foot down, then hop! It's hot.

    Good things for the ones that's got.

Another jump, now to the left.

    Everybody for hisself.

In the air, now both feet down.

    Since you black, don't stick around.

Food is gone, the rent is due,

    Curse and cry and then jump two.

All the people out of work,

    Hold for three, then twist and jerk.

Cross the line, they count you out.

    That's what hopping's all about.

Both feet flat, the game is done.

They think I lost. I think I won.

From *Just Give Me a Cool Drink of Water 'fore I Diiie*

A children's gospel choir, Harlem, New York.

POETRY

After *I Know Why the Caged Bird Sings* was published, Angelou published the first of many books of poetry, *Just Give Me a Cool Drink of Water 'fore I Diiie*. It was nominated for a Pulitzer Prize. Now, in addition to speaking English, French, Spanish, Italian, Arabic, and Fanti, Angelou spoke the language of poetry.

Poetry grew naturally from Angelou's work in theater and songwriting. Her poems often feature song-like repetitions of lines and verses as well as the rhythm of spoken language and simple word choices, including slang. Many poems rhyme rather than flow in free verse. The poems often speak in a tone of irony; that is, they mean something different from what they actually say. But despite their frequent sense of teasing and playfulness, the poems usually explore serious subjects. Like the work of other black poets, Angelou's poems address the dangers of African-American life, whether from violence, addiction, poverty, racial discrimination, injustice, or simply the waste of lost chances. They seem particularly sensitive to the dangers that challenge young people, asking young readers especially to be careful, take themselves seriously, and remember and honor the past.

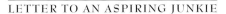

*L*et me hip you to the streets,

Jim,

Ain't nothing happening.

Maybe some tomorrows gone up in smoke,

raggedy preachers, telling a joke

to lonely, son-less old ladies' maids.

Nothing happening,

Nothing shakin', Jim.

A slough of young cats riding that

cold, white horse,

a grey old monkey on their back, of course,

does rodeo tricks.

No haps, man.

No haps.

A worn-out pimp, with a space-age conk,

setting up some fool for a game of tonk,

or poker or

get 'em dead and alive.

The streets?

Climb into the streets, man, like you climb

into the ass end of a lion.

Then it's fine.

It's a bug-a-loo and a shing-a-ling,

African dreams on a buck-and-a-wing and a prayer.

That's the streets, man,

Nothing happening.

From Just Give Me a Cool Drink of Water 'fore I Diiie

INAUGURATION

*I*n 1992, William (Bill) Jefferson Clinton was elected president of the United States. Clinton, like Angelou, had grown up in Arkansas, and he asked Maya to write a poem for his presidential inauguration. Such a request or commission is not an inaugural requirement or even a tradition, but other presidents have made them. John F. Kennedy, for example, commissioned poet Robert Frost to read a poem at his inauguration in 1960.

When Angelou read her poem "On the Pulse of Morning" at Clinton's 1993 inauguration, she was the first black woman poet to be so honored. She stood at the podium that cold January morning, a woman with no more than a high school education, and spoke her words to the privileged audience before her and to the audience listening and watching around the country.

Angelou at the 1993 presidential inauguration.

"On the Pulse of Morning" is a public poem; it addresses a collective you—in this case, the citizens of America. Those citizens, the poem notes, "each of you, a bordered country," are separate, yet the poem suggests they must somehow unite. Angelou uses the image of a river and invites her audience to come to the river "clad in peace." In a time of waste, debris, and cynicism, the poem asks its audience to care for each other, themselves, and the land. Despite the mistakes of the past, the poem urges taking steps toward change. How will those steps be taken? The ending of the poem suggests a simple beginning:

> Here, on the pulse of this new day,
> You may have the grace to look up and out
> And into your sister's eyes,
> And into your brother's face,
> Your country,
> And say simply
> Very simply
> With hope—
> Good morning.

*A*cross the wall of the world,

A River sings a beautiful song. It says,

Come, rest here by my side.

Each of you, a bordered country,

Delicate and strangely made proud,

Yet thrusting perpetually under siege.

Your armed struggles for profit

Have left collars of waste upon

My shore, currents of debris upon my breast.

Yet today I call you to my riverside,

If you will study war no more.

Come, clad in peace,

And I will sing the songs

The Creator gave to me when I and the

Tree and the Rock were one.

Before cynicism was a bloody sear across your brow

And when you yet knew you still knew nothing.

The River sang and sings on.

From "On the Pulse of Morning"

C O U R A G E

𝓑y the time Angelou delivered her poem at the presidential inauguration, she had published books of autobiography and poetry regularly for more than 20 years. She was well known as an American writer and had achieved critical and commercial success. She had settled into a personal routine for writing, which often meant isolating herself in a hotel room—regardless of where she was living—for several hours every morning, then returning home to walk, see friends, and cook, one of her favorite activities.

Yet fame and success did not protect Angelou's work, especially her poetry, from criticism. Some reviewers found fault with her poems for being too simple and using "lackluster language," easy metaphors, or clichés. In defense, other reviewers responded that Angelou's work followed a neglected oral tradition, such as slave and work songs, and carried currents of jazz, hip-hop, and the Bible.

Angelou's response was to keep working. In the 1990s, she added another writing form to her repertoire when she wrote and published several books for children. A poem published in Angelou's 1978 volume of poetry *And Still I Rise* became the text for a 1993 picture book entitled *Life Doesn't Frighten Me*, illustrated by painter Jean-Michel Basquiat. The bold images of the poem, its bad dogs, panthers, strangers, shadows, and snakes, accompanied by the repetitive assertion "Life doesn't frighten me at all," suggest the possibility of just the opposite: "Life scares me plenty of times!" The poem's real subject, of course, is courage and how people confront their fears. Angelou has confronted her fears, including whether or not her writing would be "good enough," many times.

Shadows on the wall

Noises down the hall

Life doesn't frighten me at all

Bad dogs barking loud

Big ghosts in a cloud

Life doesn't frighten me at all.

Mean old Mother Goose

Lions on the loose

They don't frighten me at all

Dragons breathing flame

On my counterpane

That doesn't frighten me at all.

I go boo

Make them shoo

I make fun

Way they run

I won't cry

So they fly

I just smile

They go wild

Life doesn't frighten me at all.

Tough guys in a fight

All alone at night

Life doesn't frighten me at all.

Panthers in the park

Strangers in the dark

No, they don't frighten me at all.

That new classroom where

Boys all pull my hair

(Kissy little girls

With their hair in curls)

They don't frighten me at all.

Don't show me frogs and snakes

And listen for my scream,

If I'm afraid at all

It's only in my dreams.

I've got a magic charm

That I keep up my sleeve,

I can walk the ocean floor

And never have to breathe.

Life doesn't frighten me at all

Not at all

Not at all.

Life doesn't frighten me at all.

From *And Still I Rise*

41

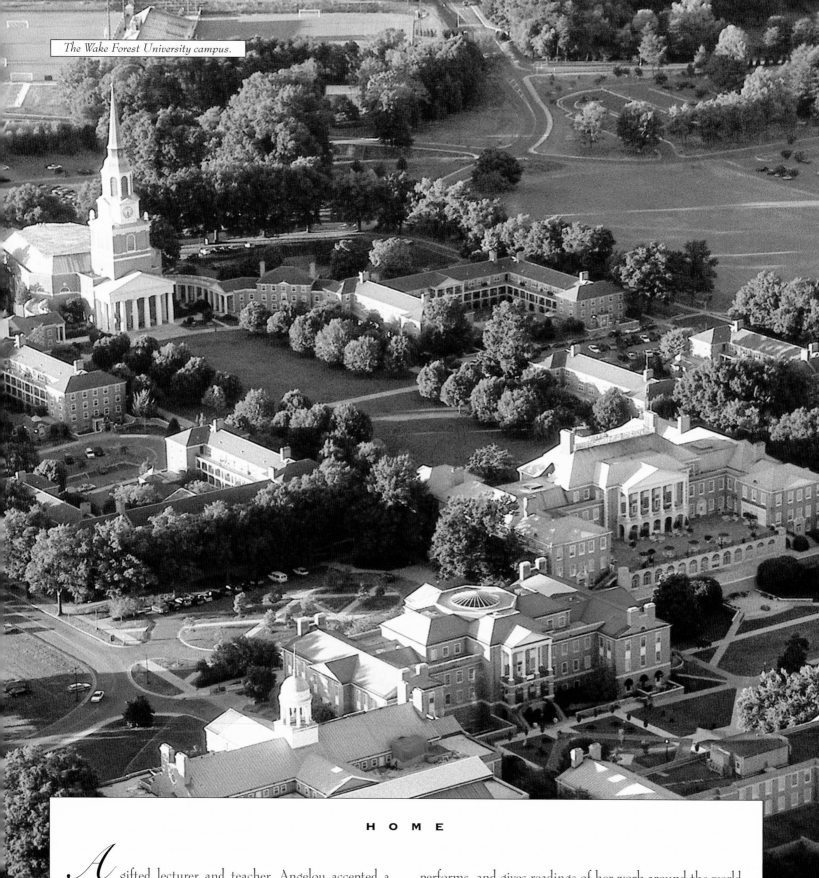

The Wake Forest University campus.

HOME

$\mathcal{A}$ gifted lecturer and teacher, Angelou accepted a lifetime appointment as the first Reynolds Professor of American Studies at Wake Forest University in Winston-Salem, North Carolina, in 1981. Although she still travels, performs, and gives readings of her work around the world, North Carolina has remained her home ever since. There she has continued to write poetry, autobiography, and essays, and to work in film, television, and theater.

Having a home is an experience that characterizes the late period of Angelou's life. In her book of essays entitled *Even the Stars Look Lonesome*, she writes, "I find that my physical ailments, which are a part of growing older, do not depress me so deeply. I find that I am quicker to laugh and much quicker to forgive. I am much happier at receiving small gifts and more delighted to be a donor of large gifts. And all of that because I am settled in my home."

By listening to her inner voice and finding a way to express what she heard, Maya Angelou has overcome the obstacles of poverty, rape, and self-doubt to accept life's gifts. For her, those gifts include the ability to bring language to the page with grace, courage, and humor, and to see that language affect a multitude of readers. Writer James Baldwin said of Angelou's book *I Know Why the Caged Bird Sings*, "I know that not since the days of my childhood, when people in books were more real than the people one saw every day, have I found myself so moved." The sixth volume of Angelou's autobiography, *A Song Flung Up to Heaven*, published in 2002, ends with Angelou beginning to write the first page of *I Know Why the Caged Bird Sings*. Clearly, settled at home, she has more to write.

ON AGING

When you see me sitting quietly,

Like a sack left on the shelf,

Don't think I need your chattering.

I'm listening to myself.

Hold! Stop! Don't pity me!

Hold! Stop your sympathy!

Understanding if you got it,

Otherwise I'll do without it!

When my bones are stiff and aching,

And my feet won't climb the stair,

I will only ask one favor:

Don't bring me no rocking chair.

When you see me walking, stumbling,

Don't study and get it wrong.

'Cause tired don't mean lazy

And every goodbye ain't gone.

I'm the same person I was back then,

A little less hair, a little less chin,

A lot less lungs and much less wind.

But ain't I lucky I can still breathe in.

From *And Still I Rise*

ACKNOWLEDGMENTS

Photo Credits

Corbis (Bettman, Sophie Bassouls/Sygma, Christopher Felver, Allen Ginsberg, Brasz Marc, Leif Skoogfors,
Brian A.Vikander, Michael S. Yamashita)

Getty Images/Time Life Pictures (Will McIntyre)

Hulton/Archive Photos (Edward A. Hausner, Sheldon Hire, Gene Lester, Stephen Matterson Jr./New York Times,
Carl Mydans, Orlando, Arnie Sachs, Washington Bureau)

North Wind Picture Archive, Wake Forest University

Poetry & Prose Credits

"Harlem Hopscotch" and "Letter to an Aspiring Junkie" from Just Give Me a Cool Drink of Water 'fore I Diiie
by Maya Angelou, copyright © 1971 by Maya Angelou. Used by permission of Random House, Inc.

"Come. And Be My Baby" and "Song for the Old Ones" by Maya Angelou, copyright © 1975 by Maya Angelou, from Oh Pray My
Wings Are Gonna Fit Me Well by Maya Angelou, copyright © 1975 by Maya Angelou. Used by permission of Random House, Inc.

"Life Doesn't Frighten Me," "On Aging," and "Still I Rise" by Maya Angelou, copyright © 1978 by Maya Angelou, from And Still I
Rise by Maya Angelou, copyright © 1978 by Maya Angelou. Used by permission of Random House, Inc.

"A Good Woman Feeling Bad" by Maya Angelou, copyright © 1983 by Maya Angelou, from Shaker, Why Don't You Sing?
by Maya Angelou, copyright © 1983 by Maya Angelou. Used by permission of Random House, Inc.

"On the Pulse of Morning" (18-line excerpt) from On the Pulse of Morning
by Maya Angelou, copyright © 1993 by Maya Angelou. Used by permission of Random House, Inc.

Chapter 1 excerpt from I Know Why the Caged Bird Sings
by Maya Angelou, copyright © 1969 and renewed 1997 by Maya Angelou. Used by permission of Random House, Inc.

Chapter 6 excerpts from The Heart of a Woman
by Maya Angelou, copyright © 1981 by Maya Angelou. Used by permission of Random House, Inc.

SELECTED WORKS BY MAYA ANGELOU

Poetry

Just Give Me a Cool Drink of Water 'fore I Diiie, 1971

Oh Pray My Wings Are Gonna Fit Me Well, 1975

And Still I Rise, 1978

Shaker, Why Don't You Sing?, 1983

I Shall Not Be Moved, 1990

On the Pulse of Morning, 1993

The Complete Collected Poems of Maya Angelou, 1994

Soul Looks Back in Wonder, 1994

Prose

I Know Why the Caged Bird Sings, 1970

Gather Together in My Name, 1974

Singin' and Swingin' and Gettin' Merry Like Christmas, 1976

The Heart of a Woman, 1981

All God's Children Need Traveling Shoes, 1986

Wouldn't Take Nothing for My Journey Now, 1993

Even the Stars Look Lonesome, 1997

A Song Flung Up to Heaven, 2002

SELECTED WORKS BY MAYA ANGELOU

CHILDREN'S BOOKS

Life Doesn't Frighten Me, 1993

My Painted House, My Friendly Chicken, and Me, 1994

Kofi and His Magic, 1996

INDEX

Published by Creative Education
123 South Broad Street, Mankato, Minnesota 56001
Creative Education is an imprint of The Creative Company
Copyright © 2004 Creative Education
Illustrations copyright © 2004 John Thompson
International copyrights reserved in all countries.
No part of this book may be reproduced in any form without
written permission from the publisher.
Art direction by Rita Marshall; Design by Stephanie Blumenthal
Printed in Italy.
Library of Congress Cataloging-in-Publication Data
Angelou, Maya.
Maya Angelou / [compiled] by Patricia Kirkpatrick.
p. cm. — (Voices in poetry)
Summary: Examines the life and accomplishments of the African-
American writer, performer, and teacher. Includes a selection of her
poetry.
ISBN 1-58341-281-6
1. Children's poetry, American. [1. Angelou, Maya. 2. Authors,
American. 3. Poets, American. 4. African Americans—Biography.
5. Women—Biography. 6. American poetry.] I. Kirkpatrick,
Patricia. II. Title. III. Voices in poetry (Mankato, Minn.)
PS3551.N464A6 2003   811'.54—dc21   2002035125

First Edition
9 8 7 6 5 4 3 2 1